500
HILARIOUS
PICK UP LINES

HONEY
HUMOUR

1) I hope you know CPR, because you just took my breath away

2) So, aside from taking my breath away, what do you do for a living?

3) I ought to complain to Spotify for you not being named this week's hottest single

4) If you were a vegetable, you'd be a 'cute-cumber'

5) Are you a parking ticket? Because you've got FINE written all over you

6) Do you believe in love at first sight, or should I walk by again?

7) Feel my shirt. Know what it's made of? Boyfriend material.

8) Know what's on the menu? Me 'n' u.

9) Are you a magician? Because when I'm looking at you, you make everyone else disappear!

10) Are you a camera? Because I look at you and smile!

11) Is your dad a boxer? Because you're a knockout!

12) They say nothing lasts forever. So would you be my nothing?

13) Are you a broom? Because you've swept me off my feet!

14) I'm no mathematician, but I've been told I'm good with numbers. How about you give me yours so I can prove it?

15) You must be made of Copper and Tellurium — because you're CuTe!

16) Life without you is like a broken pencil... pointless

17) Something's wrong with my eyes, because I can't take them off you

18) Somebody better call God, because he's missing an angel

19) Do you have a map? I keep getting lost in your eyes

20) I'm sorry, were you talking to me? No? Would you like to?

21) I believe in following my dreams. Can I have your Instagram?

22) I'm not usually religious, but when I saw you, I knew you were the answer to my prayers

23) Good thing I have my library card... because I'm checking you out

24) Your hand looks heavy, let me hold it for you

25) Kiss me if I'm wrong but dinosaurs still exist right?

26) Are you Google? Because you have everything I'm searching for

27) Are you related to Yoda? Because yoda-licious

28) Let's flip a coin! Heads, you're mine. Tails, I'm yours!

29) Let's commit the perfect crime. I'll steal your heart. You steal mine

30) I'm good at Algebra. I can replace your X and you wouldn't need to figure out Y

31) I'm no photographer, but I can picture us together

32) Why would I need to know about the solar system? My whole world revolves around you

33) Are you a beaver? Because daaaam

34) This may be cheesy... but I I think you're grate

35) Is your name Wi-Fi? Because I'm feeling a connection

36) I like your last name. Can I have it?

37) Summer's over... Because you're about to fall for me

38) You're single. I'm single. Coincidence? I think not

39) You know what's faster than the speed of light? My heart when I think of you

40) I'm lost. Can you tell me which road leads to your heart?

41) Do you have a fever? You just look hot to me

42) I'm learning about important dates in history. Wanna be one of them?

43) Are you the moon? Because even when it's dark, you still seem to shine

44) Can you call a lifeguard? Because I'm drowning in your eyes

45) Are you a dictionary? Cause you add meaning to my life

46) Have you been fishing before? I think we should hook up

47) Do you like science? Because I've got my ion you

48) There's something wrong with my phone... It doesn't have your number in it

49) If you were a burger at McDonalds, you'd be a McGorgeous

50) Are you a volcano? Because I lava you

51) I must be in a museum, because you are a work of art

52) Are you a campfire? Because you're hot and I want S'more

53) If I were a little lamb, would you marry me?

54) I'm no organ donor but I'd be happy to give you my heart

53) You know, if a fat man with a beard happens to stuff you in a bag one night, don't be afraid — I told Santa that I want you for Christmas this year

56) You're legs must be tired because you've been running through my mind all night

57) Do you like Nintendo? Because Wii would look good together

58) I don't believe in love at first sight, but I'll make an exception for you

59) Do you play football? Because you're a keeper!

60) You must be a high test score because I want to to you home and show to my mother

61) Charizards are red, Squirtles are blue. If you were a Pokemon, I'd choose you!

62) Do you have a band-aid? Cause I scrapped my knees falling for you

63) If I had a penny for every time I though of you, I'd have exactly once cent because you never leave my mind

64) If I were a cat, I'd spend all 9 lives with you

65) Are you a 90 degree angle? Because you lookin' right

66) Guess what I'm wearing... the smile you gave me

67) If you were a Transformer, you'd be Optimus Fine

68) Do you like French Food? How about I give you a quiche

69) Do you wanna go to the gym? Because I can see you and me working out

70) I like legos, you like legos. Why don't we build a relationship?

71) Well, I'm here! What are your other two wishes?

72) Excuse me, I think you dropped something... my jaw

73) Hey, tie your shoes! I don't you falling for anyone else

74) Are you a time-traveler? Because I see you in my future!

75) I'd never play hide and seek with you, because someone like you is impossible to find

76) Are you a keyboard? Because you're just my type

77) Are you a bank loan? Because you got my interest

78) Did it hurt when you fell from the vending machine? Because you're a snack

79) I thought there were only 21 letters in the alphabet, but then I realized that I forgot U R A Q T

80) Do you have a name, or can I call you Mine?

81) Do you like vegetables? Because I love you from my head tomatoes

82) If you were a triangle, you'd be acute one

83) Are you craving pizza? Because I'd love to get a pizza you

84) If you were a fruit, you'd be a fineapple

85) If a star fell for every time I thought of you, the sky would be empty

86) Are you Australian? Because you meet all of my koala-fications

87) If I had a garden, I'd put your tulips and my tulips together

88) I thought happiness starts with H. But why does mine start with U?

89) When a penguin finds a mate, they stay with them for the rest of their life. Will you be my penguin?

90) Hey, my name's Microsoft. Can I crash at your place tonight?

91) You must be a ninja, because you snuck into my heart

92) Your lips look so lonely... would they like to meet mine?

93) You spend so much time in my mind... I should charge you rent

94) Did you drink soda? Because you look so-da-licious

95) I'd show you my world, but I'm sure you own a mirror

96) You look cold. Want to use me as a blanket?

97) I'd like to take you to the movies, but they don't let you bring in your own snacks

98) You're like the lyrics to my favorite song... hard to forget and always on my mind

99) Forget about Spiderman, Superman and Batman. I'll be your man

100) Your eyes have told me a lot of things. The only thing they haven't told me is your name

101) I was looking in the widow of a store and I saw something adorable to get you for Christmas. Then I realized it was my reflection

102) Kissing is the language of love, so how about a conversation?

103) Do you have a license? Because you're driving me crazy

104) Are you an overdue book? Because you have fine written all over you!

105) Can I take your picture to prove to all my friends that angels do exist?

106) If you hold 8 roses in front of a mirror, you'd see 9 of the most beautiful things in the world!

107) On a scale of 1 to 10, You're a 9 and I'm the 1 you need

108) I am going to punch you in the mouth... with my own mouth. Softly, because I like you

109) Are you Ariel? Because we mermaid for each other

110) You may fall from the sky, you may fall from a tree, but the best way to fall... is to fall in love with me

111) You wanna know what's the best thing in my life? It's the first word of this sentence

112) You're pretty and I'm cute. Together, we'd be pretty cute

113) Are you Christmas? Because I wanna Merry you

114) I just wanna c_ddle, but I can't because I'm missing U

115) Are you from China? Because I'm China get your number

116) You must be a tornado, because you just blew me away!

117) People call me John, but you can call me Tonight!

118) If you like water, then you already like 72% of me

119) You must be made of Fluorine, Iodine and Neon because you're so FINe!

120) Do you like sleeping? Me, too! We should do it together sometime.

121) You look familiar. Did we have class together? I could've sworn we had Chemistry

122) My friend over there really wants your number so they know where to get a hold of me in the morning

123) I know what you should be for Halloween. Mine

124) You know what's beautiful? Read the first word again

125) That's weird, I've never seen a princess out of her castle

126) You must be the square root of two, because I feel irrational around you

127) Do you know that I'm a scientist, and you are my lab?

128) Can I borrow a kiss? I promise to give it back

129) Do you like raisins? How do you feel about a date?

130) Are you from Tennessee? Because you're the only 10 I see!

131) Roses are red, violets are blue. I didn't know what perfect was until I met you

132) If you were words on a page, you'd be fine print

133) I must be a snowflake, because I've fallen for you

134) I know you're busy right today, but can you add me to your to-do list?

135) If you were a steak, you would be well done

136) Does your name start with "C"? Because I can C us together

137) Have you always been this cute, or did you have to work at it?

138) Are you a cat? Because I'm feline a connection between us

139) Is your last name Gillette? Because you are the best a man can get

140) I'll give you a kiss. If you don't like it, you can return it

141) If I was the judge, I'd sentence you to life by my side

142) That shirt looks great on you!... As a matter of fact, so would I

143) You must be yogurt, because I want to spoon you

144) Are you an exam? Because I have been studying you like crazy

145) Is there an airport nearby or is it my heart taking off?

146) The only problem with your lips is that they're too far away from mine

147) How many times should I walk by you before you realize we're meant to be?

148) How much longer until I get to the part where you give me your number?

149) I seem to have lost my phone number. Can I have yours?

150) For some reason, I was feeling a little off today. But when you came along, you definitely turned me on

151) Was your father an alien? Because there's nothing like you on Earth!

152) I'm sorry, were you talking to me?... Well then, please start

153) Sorry, but you owe me a drink because when I looked at you, I dropped mine

154) You are like my favorite cup of coffee, hot and lip-smacking!

155) Your body is a wonderland, and I want to be Alice

156) If I had a star for every time you brightened my day, I'd have a galaxy in my hand

157) I'm not a hoarder, but I really want to keep you forever

158) Is that a mistletoe above your head or are you about to kiss me?

159) Are you an artist? Because you're really good at drawing me in

160) If I had four quarters to give to the cutest guys in the world, you would have a dollar!

161) Are you HTTP? Because without you, I'm just ://

162) You must be debt, because my interest in you is growing

163) Baby, our love is like dividing by zero —
it cannot be defined

164) If you were a chicken, you'd be im-peck-able!

165) We're not socks but I think we'd make a great pair

166) I would say God bless you, but it looks like he already did

167) Are you an alien? Because you just abducted my heart

168) Did it hurt when you fell from heaven?

169) Kissing burns 6 calories a minute. Wanna workout together?

170) Can I borrow a quarter? I want to call my mom and tell her I just met the girl of my dreams

171) My buddies bet me that I wouldn't be able to start a conversation with the hottest person in the bar. Wanna buy some drinks with their money?

172) Are you an omelette? Because you're making me egg-cited!

173) You're my Bluetooth device. Thanks for pairing with me!

174) I was trying to send you something cute, but I don't think I can fit you in this text box

175) Did you invent the airplane? Cause you seem Wright for me

176) Are you Mexican? Because you're my Juan and only!

177) Hi, I'm Mr. Right. Someone said you were looking for me?

178) Damn, if being sexy was a crime, you'd be guilty as charged!

179) You must be the guy who's going to buy me a drink

180) Are you a banana? Because I find you a-peeling

181) Put down that cupcake... you're sweet enough already

182) Four plus four equals eight, but you plus me equals fate

183) Are you sure you're not from South Korea? Because I'm sure you're my 'Seoul'-mate

184) Excuse me, I think you have something in your eye. Oh wait, it's just a sparkle!

185) No wonder the sky is grey today, all the blue is in your eyes

186) Would you allow me Dubai you a drink?

187) Is your name Dunkin? Because I Donut want to spend another day without you

188) Call me Shrek because I'm head ogre heels for you

189) You're not a vegetarian, are you? Because I'd love to meat you

190) Is your name Dwayne Johnson? Because you Rock my world!

191) You're so sweet, you'd put Hershey's out of business

192) I play the field, and it looks like I just hit a home run with you

193) My doctor says I could use more Vitamin U

194) If your heart was a prison, I would like to be sentenced for life

195) You know what you would look really beautiful in? My arms

196) If you were a potato, you'd be a sweet one

197) You're like a fine wine. The more of you I drink in, the better I feel

198) Are you a cat? Because you are purrrfect

199) We should get some coffee sometime, because I like you a latte

200) You be the Dairy Queen and I'll be your Burger King: You treat me right, and I'll do it your way

201) Are you a doughnut? Because I find you a-dough-rable!

202) I need some answers for my math homework. Quick! What's your number?

203) I think we'd make a cute pear

204) I sneezed because God blessed me with you

205) You've stolen a pizza my heart

206) If I was an octopus, all my 3 hearts would beat for you

207) I think you're barbe-cute

208) See these keys? I wish I had the one to your heart

209) I think we are mint to be!

210) You're the only girl I love now... but in ten years, I'll love another girl. She'll call you 'Mommy.'

211) Are you a carbon sample? Because I want to date you!

212) I'm sorry, I don't think we've met. I wouldn't forget a pretty face like that

213) Hey gorgeous, will you be my Tinderella?

214) If I were a stoplight, I'd turn every time you pass by just so I could stare at you a bit longer

215) I've been looking for you since I heard my first fairytale

216) Was than an earthquake, or did you just rock my world?

217) You breathe oxygen, too? We have so much in common

218) Excuse me, but I'm new in town. Can I have the directions to your place?

219) I'm no electrician, but I can light up your day

220) Do you need a place to stay? My heart is open for you

221) If you were a pill, I'd overdose

222) You've got everything I've been searching for, and believe me— I've been looking for a long time

223) If you were a song, you'd be the best track on the album

224) Your eyes are blue like the ocean. And baby, I'm lost at sea

225) Hey, don't frown. You never know who could be falling in love with your smile

226) Did you just come out of the oven? Because you're hot

227) I don't know which is prettier today — the weather, or your eyes

228) In my opinion, there three kinds of beautiful: cute, pretty, and sexy. Somehow, you manage to be all three

229) Are you an N95 mask? Because I want you on my face

230) Would you mind giving me a pinch? You're so cute, I must be dreaming

231) When I text you goodnight later, what phone number should I use?

232) I'd say you're the bomb, but that could turn into lethal conversation

233) You must be a hell of a thief, because you managed to steal my heart from across the room

234) It this the Hogwarts Express? Because it feels like you and I are headed somewhere magical

235) I like gold, but "A" is silent

236) There's plenty of fish in the sea, but you're the only one I'd like to catch

237) Do you like Mexican food? Because I want to wrap you in my arms and make you my Bae-ritto

238) I love you with all my circle, not my heart. Because hearts can stop beating, but a circle goes on forever

239) Were your parents Greek gods? Because it takes two gods to make a goddess

240) I'll be yours forever. Just tell me when to start

241) If you were a basketball, I'd never shoot. Because I'd always miss you

242) Your eyes are like the sunset, hard to turn away from

243) Are you a fruit, because Honeydew you know how fine you look right now?

244) You are my compass. Without you, I'm lost

245) You look like a cold glass of refreshing water, and I am the thirstiest man in the world

246) Sorry for staring, I think your face is a work of art

247) You must be an essential textbook passage because seeing you is the highlight of my day

248) Are you an alien? Because you're out of this world

249) I know where they give out free drinks... It's a place called "My House"!

250) I'm going to have to ask you to leave. You're making the other women look bad

251) Were you arrested earlier? It's gotta be illegal to look that good

252) You know, we were born without clothes

253) Hey babe, my love is a tidal wave and you're beach front property

254) Are you a florist? Because ever since I met you, my life has been so Rosy

255) They told me never to judge a book by its cover but I don't even know you and I am already checking you out

256) Your body must be made of oxygen and neon because you are the ONe

257) If I had to choose between breathing or loving you, I would say "I love you" with my last breath

258) Excuse me but are you a guitar? Because I'd definitely pick you

259) Did you have lucky charms for breakfast? Because you look magically delicious

260) I googled your name earlier... I clicked on "I'm Feeling Lucky"

261) I hope there's a fire truck nearby, cause you're smokin'!

262) Albert Einstein believed that nothing was faster than light. But he wasn't here to see how fast I feel for you

263) I used to be able to recite the English alphabet before we met. Now, I can't get past "U"

264) Are you a phone charger? Because without you, I'd die

265) If you were a flower, you'd be damnnn-delion

266) Wanna exchange genetic information with me?

267) You remind me of a magnet, because you sure are attracting me over here!

268) Are you on Nickelodeon? Because you're a-Dora-ble!

269) Roses are red, violets are blue. How would you like it if I came home with you?

270) I will stop loving you when an apple grows from a mango tree on the 30th of February

271) They say Disney is the happiest place on Earth. Well, no one has ever been standing next to you

272) You had me at "Hello World"

273) My love for you is like diarrhea, I just can't hold it in

274) Your smile lit up the room, so I just had to come over

275) You are more special than relativity

276) Hey, you can't spell Calculus without "us"

277) I used to be a gambler, but then I realized that all I needed was the Queen of my Heart

278) You must be a pile of dinosaur bones, because I dig you

279) Hey girl, did we just share electrons? Because I'm feeling a covalent bond between us

280) Do you live in a cornfield? Because I'm stalking you

281) You still use Internet Explorer? You must like it nice and slow

282) Please call 9-1-1, because you just made my heart stop!

283) It's not my fault I fell for you. You tripped me

284) Are you made of beryllium, gold, and titanium? Because you are BeAuTi-ful

285) Do you sit on a pile of glitter? Because you always keep shining

286) Does your father sell diamonds? Because you are FLAWLESS!

287) If you were an eBay auction, I'd totally 'Buy it Now'

288) Blue eyes, red lips, pale face. So pretty. You look like the flag of France

289) If beauty were time, you would be forever

290) Remember me? Oh, that's right, I've only met you in my dreams

291) I want to be your teardrop, so I could be born in your eyes, live on your cheeks, and die on your lips

292) My favourite element on the periodic table is Uranium, because I am in love with U

293) I think the gaps between my fingers were meant for yours

294) My name isn't Elmo, but you can tickle me any time you want to

295) Baby, I might not be a Sriracha sauce but I sure will spice up your life

296) You must be a star, because I can't stop orbiting around you

297) They say dating is a numbers game... so can I get your number?

298) My lips are like skittles. Wanna taste the rainbow?

299) Baby, I'm no Fred Flintstone, but I can make your Bedrock

300) I wish I was your coronary artery so that I could be wrapped around your heart

301) Damn girl, I thought diamonds were pretty until I laid my eyes on you!

302) Vogue just called. They want to put you on the cover

303) Are you made out of grapes? Because you are as fine as wine!

304) I wish you were broadband, so I could get high-speed access

305) My heart forgets to beat the moment I see you

306) Even if there were no gravity, I'd still fall for you

307) The letter 'X' scares me, because I never want to be yours

308) Hey girl, are you gold? Because I'm in Au of your beauty

309) Why would I want to look at the stars when I can look in your eyes?

310) Are your parents bakers? Because you're a cutie pie

311) Are you Netflix? Because I could watch you for hours

314) Is there a science room nearby, or am I just sensing chemistry between us?

315) You are like the best coffee: tall, dark and strong

316) You must be made of cheese, because you're looking Gouda tonight!

317) I may not be good at dancing, but I can tangle with you all night long

318) Your homepage, or mine?

319) I'm writing a term paper on the finer things in life, and I was wondering if I could interview you

320) Are you cake? Because I want a piece of that

321) Can you take me to the doctor? Because I just broke my leg falling for you

322) Did you hear about the new disease called 'beautiful'? I think you're infected!

323) Hello, Cupid called. He wants to tell you that he needs my heart back

324) I value my breath, so it would be nice if you didn't take it away every time you walk past

325) Is there a rainbow today? Because I just found the treasure I've been searching for!

326) You're so sweet, you're giving me a toothache

327) Hi, my name's Chance. Do I have one?

328) There's a side view, a rearview, and you know what else? I love-view

329) Stop, drop, and roll, baby. You are on fire

330) Do you think we'd look cute on a wedding cake together?

331) So what do you do? Other than make women fall for you all day

332) Are you lost, miss? Because heaven is a long way from here

333) Could you please step away from the bar? You're melting all the ice!

334) Do you work at NASA? I think you beauty is out of this world

335) Please stop looking so attractive. I'm trying to stop liking you

336) Please keep your distance, I might fall for you

337) Is your dad a preacher? Because girl, you're a blessing!

338) I know someone who likes you, If I wasn't so shy, I'd tell you who

339) To know me is to love me. Are you ready to get to know me?

340) If I told you that you had a nice body, would you hold it against me?

341) Is your nickname Chapstick? Because you're da balm!

342) My name may not be Luna, but I sure know how to Lovegood!

343) Are you the cure for Alzheimer's? Because you're unforgettable!

344) Did the sun just come out, or did you just smile at me?

345) I've had a terrible day, and it always makes me feel better to see a pretty girl smile. So, would you smile for me?

346) Do you know Karate? Because your body is kickin'!

347) If you don't reply in three seconds, you're mine

348) When I look into your eyes, it is like a gateway into the world of which I want to be a part

349) You are so beautiful, I wish I could plant you and grow a whole field of you!

350) Roses are red, bananas are yellow, wanna go out with a nice little fellow?

351) I may not be a genie, but I can make your dreams come true

352) Are you my appendix? Because I have a funny feeling in my stomach that makes me feel like I should take you out

353) Can you kiss me on the cheek so I can at least say a cute girl kissed me tonight?

354) Are you a girl scout? Because you tie my heart in knots

355) You may not be my first, but you can be my last

356) Excuse me, is your name Earl Grey? Because you look like a hot-tea!

357) I have a pen. You have a phone number. Think of the possibilities

358) I do not think much. I do not think often. But when I do, it's always about you

359) When I first you, I looked for a signature because every masterpiece has one

360) Hi, do you have a few minutes for me to hit on you?

361) Do you have a pencil? Because I want to erase your past and write our future

362) You're hotter than Papa Bear's porridge

363) I don't know your name, but I'm sure it is as beautiful as you are

364) Your lips are kind of wrinkled. Mind if I press them?

365) Are you a microwave? Because you melt my heart

366) Going to bed? Mind if I Slytherin?

367) Just so you know, I'm not flirting with you. I'm just being extra nice to you since you're extra attractive

368) Of all your beautiful curves, your smile is my favourite

369) If you were Sprite, I'd obey my thirst!

370) Hello, this is me making the first move. Your turn

371) Hey, stranger. Stop being a stranger.

372) When I'm older, I'll look back at all of my crowning memories, and I'll think of the day my children were born, the day I got married, and the day that I met you

373) I may not be the best looking guy here, but I am the only one talking to you

374) First, I was playing hard to get. Now, you're playing hard to forget

375) My friends bet I can't talk to the prettiest girl. Wanna use their money to buy drinks?

376) Do you smoke pot? Because weed be cute together

377) Do you believe in love at first text, or should I text you again?

378) You're that "Nothing" when people ask me what I'm thinking about

379) You know, Sweetie, my lips won't just kiss themselves

380) Your one-time PIN is 143. For your protection, do not share this code with anyone. Enter this code to confirm your love for me.

381) If you were ground coffee, you'd be Espresso cause you're so fine

382) Falling for you would be a very short trip

383) If beauty were time, you would definitely be an eternity

384) I just had to come to talk with you. Sweetness is my weakness

385) Are you from Russia? Because you're Russian my heart rate!

386) If you were a tear in my eye, I would not cry for fear of losing you

387) If loving me is wrong, you don't wanna be right

388) I might need crutches. You make my knees weak

389) Do you have a bandage? I skinned my knee falling for you

390) When I look at you, I feel like I'm a pirate and just found my buried treasure

391) You're like the wind... because you blow me away!

392) If beauty was a grain of sand, you'd be a thousand beaches

393) Is your name John? Because I've never Cena girl like you before

394) You must be a compound of barium and beryllium, because you're a total Babe

395) Call the CDC! Your smile is contagious

396) You know what you and planet Earth have in common? You're both getting hotter each year

397) I must be psychic, because I see you in my future

398) Hey, excuse me! You have a bit of cuteness on your face

399) I bet dentists hate you, because you're so sweet!

400) My mom told me life was like a deck of cards. So, you must be the queen of hearts

401) I've got all these fork and knives. Now, all I need is a little spoon

402) Do you ever go to the kitchen and realize you're the tastiest snack you have?

403) You're like the Renaissance after the Dark Ages... you light up my world

404) With all this electricity between us, you must be Zeus

405) The only thing more contagious than COVID-19 is your smile

406) I've got 1-ply, I've got 2-ply. But all I really want is your reply

407) Are your eyes Ikea? Because I'm lost in them

408) Do you like reptiles? Because iguana be with you

409) Do you like Harry Potter? Because I a-dumbledore you

410) Do you have 11 protons? Because you're sodium fine

411) Are you coffee? Because I've bean thinking about you a latte

412) Are you garbage? Because I want to take you out

413) Let's be nothing because nothing lasts forever

414) I will love you till a mute man tells his deaf friend about a blind man that saw a guy with no legs waling on water

415) Are you a chocolate pudding? Because I want to spoon you

416) Do you like cats, because you can take meowt on a date

417) I'm not a morning person. But if I woke up every morning next to you, I would be

418) If kisses were snowflakes, I'd send you a blizzard

419) A boy gives a girl 12 roses. Eleven real, one fake and he says to her "I will stop loving you when all the roses die"

420) So, do you have a new years resolution? Because I'm looking at mine right now

421) I just wanted to show this rose how incredibly beautiful you are!

422) I don't know how I'll ever get to class on time when it's so easy to get lost in your eyes

423) Can you pull this heart-shaped arrow out of my chest? Some little kid with wings shot me

424) We're like Little Caesar's, we're Hot 'n Ready

425) Something tells me you're sweet. Can I have a taste?

426) If I was a Jedi, would you be my force?

427) What do you and the weather have in common? You're both hot!

428) I'm a man of few words. You are beautiful, would you like to go out?

429) Is your dad a jewel thief? Because you're a real jem

430) Somebody needs to call the bomb squad, because you're the bomb!

431) I'm invisible... Oh, can you see me? How about tomorrow night?

432) Our breakup is worse than the traffic in New York. I can't move on!

433) There are 20 angels in the world: 11 are playing, 8 are sleeping and one of them is standing in front of me

434) Are you a crayon? Because you bring color to my life

435) If love was written on every grain of sand in the Sahara desert, that still doesn't equal my love for you

436) Santa's lap isn't the only place wishes come true

437) Did you hear that? Was that canon fire? Oh no, it's just my heart pounding!

438) If you were a Transformer, you'd be a HOT-obot

439) Are we related? Do you want to be?

440) There are 30 billion grains of sand on this beach, but there's only one you

441) You're like an exposed electrical wire... hot and dangerous

442) You and I are so perfect, want to make a complete circuit?

443) I was so enchanted by your beauty that I ran into that wall. So I am going to need your name and number for insurance purposes

444) Forget hydrogen, you're my number one element

445) Are you the square root of -1? Because you can't be real

446) You must be the acid to my litmus paper because every time I meet you, I turn bright red

447) If I was an enzyme, I'd be helicase so I could unzip your genes

448) I'm not being obtuse, but you're acute girl

449) Your name must be Andromeda, because we are destined to collide

450) Me without you is like a nerd without braces, a shoe without laces, aSentenceWithoutSpaces

451) I'm not staring, I'm just stuck in a loop

452) Baby, every time I see you, my cardiovascular system gets all worked up

453) You're hotter than a Bunsen burner

454) If I freeze, it's not a computer virus. I was just stunned by your beauty

455) Urkuk lu Stalga. That's Klingon for "I love you baby"

456) You're so beautiful you made me forget my pickup line

457) Do I know you? Because you look a lot like my next girlfriend

458) I'd marry your cat just to get in the family

459) Hey, do you play Center? Because are the center of my attention!

460) I don't play football, but you're my goal

461) I like Ronaldo, but I'd like to get Messi

462) Babe, you played a good match! But you and me are a perfect match

463) Are you an egg? Because the moment I see you, my smile turns sunny side up

464) If you're the pizza pie, then I'm the pizza sauce... Because I'm all over you

465) There was a girl eyeing me over there, but I'm not interested because cheese not you

466) The barista may have forgotten your name, but I sure won't

467) So would you like a soft drink, beer, maybe wine? Or would you just like my number?

468) Here's $10. Drink until I am really good looking, then come and talk to me

469) Girl, I'd like to take you out but it won't be the Last Supper

470) Are you the Easter bunny? 'Cause you've been hopping around my mind all day

471) I'm like a Christmas present, you'll love waking up to me in the morning

472) I'm Dublin my efforts to get you to go out with me

473) Can you hold my gloves for a second? I was gonna warm them by the fireplace, but you are way hotter

474) I'm sorry I didn't get you chocolates for Valentine's Day, but if you want something sweet, I'm right here

475) I know I don't have a chance, but I just wanted to hear an angel speak

476) I should have dressed up as a ghost tonight, so I could let you under my sheets

477) If you think I'm hot now, wait until you see what I turn into at midnight

478) If you were a tree, you'd be an evergreen... because I bet you look this good year-round

479) I just got this naughty list from Santa and I'm pretty sure you're on it

480) You must be from Quebec, because my feelings for you are Mont-real

481) If you were a transplant surgeon, I'd give you my heart

482) If looks could kill, you'd be a weapon of mass destruction

483) If we were playing poker, I would go all in

484) Do you like sales? Because if you're looking for one, clothing is 100% off at my place

485) If I were a fan in your room, it'd be impossible for you to turn me off

486) If you were a booger, I'd pick you first

487) Are you my homework? Because I'm not doing you but I definitely should be

488) Is your father a florist? Because you have made my life rosy

489) Are you a planet? Because you look like a heavenly body

490) The only hotter thing on my dinner table than you is Tabasco

491) Have a date with me if I'm wrong but it is still the Ice Age, isn't it?

492) Do you know the best thing about kisses? If you don't like them, you can always return them

493) You must be a small amount of red phosphorus and I must be a tiny wooden stick... because we're a match!

494) Are you a gardener? Because I like your tulips

495) If being in love was illegal, would you be my partner in crime?

496) Do you ever wear fishnets? Because you're a real catch!

497) My love for you is like copied assignment, I just can't explain it

498) You could spam me all night and I will wouldn't unsubscribe

499) Are you epinephrine? Because baby, you make my heart race

500) I don't need to look at more data. What I'm feeling with you is already statistically significant

Printed in Great Britain
by Amazon